Ages 3+

WONDER MAGIC NUMBERS

Practice Workbook For Preschoolers

Vanishing Ink | Reusable in 15 minutes | Thick Paper

1 ONE

1 1 1 1 1 1

1 1 1 1

2 TWO

2 2 2 2 2

3 THREE

3 3 3 3 3

3 3 3

Wonder House

Includes penholder,

Note I:

Extra-thick paper, no curling, the product uses the groove design to constrain the user's writing habits, use the special faded stylus pen, the writing will disappear automatically after writing, the basic handwriting is gone, the front handwriting has disappeared, no need to wait, Reusable, environmentally friendly and energy efficient.

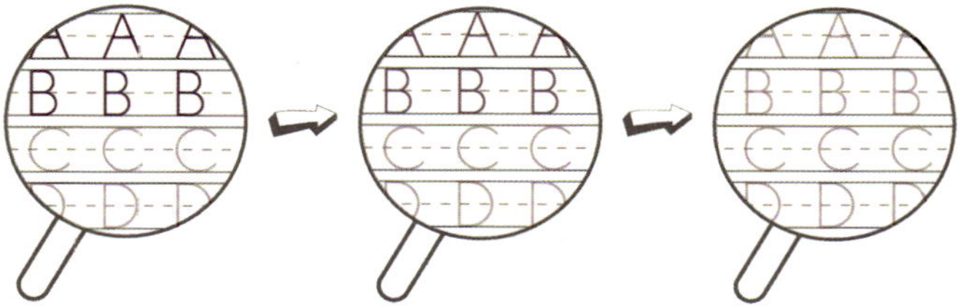

Note2:

This product is forbidden to wipe with force. Do not wipe with a damp cloth. Please keep it in a dry and ventilated place.

Note3:

1. Only use the special pen core for the product to write, the handwriting will disappear.
2. When the special pen core is in use, the ink may be clogged. Use the pen tip to lightly write several times on ordinary white paper, After the ink is smooth, then start the practice.
3. As the ink is specially processed, the handwriting will disappear after writ ng. Please do not use it for daily writing, record important information and sign documents, so as to avoid unnecessary losses to you.

Learn to Write Numbers

Draw a circle,
don't you stop
like a hero.
Then you get a zero.

One is fun!
Straight down
and then you're done.

Look and Read

Learn to Write Numbers

Around and back
on a railroad track.
You made a two
Just like that.

Around the tree,
around the tree
that's the way
to make a three.

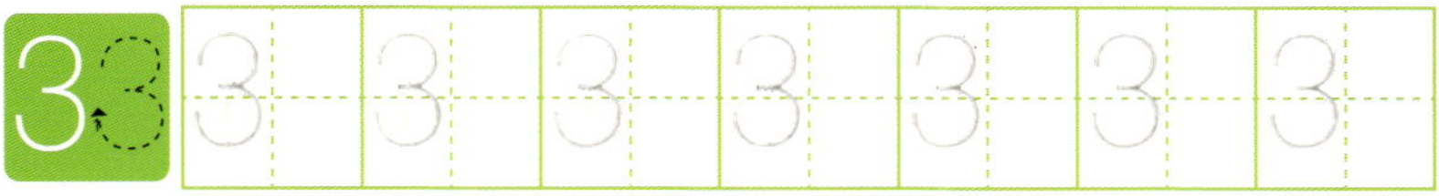

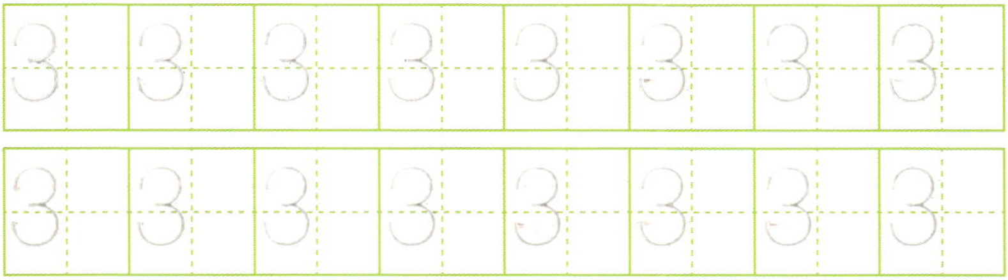

Application

Count and write correct number in the circle.

Learn to Write Numbers

Down and over,
then down some more.
that is how
you make a four.

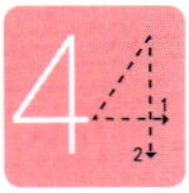

Go across
Then take a dive.
Around the bend,
And that's a five.

Application

Count and match.

1

2

3

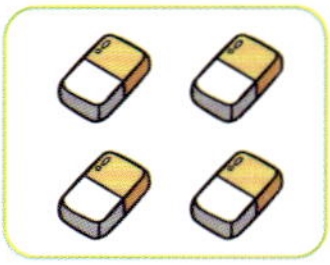

4

5

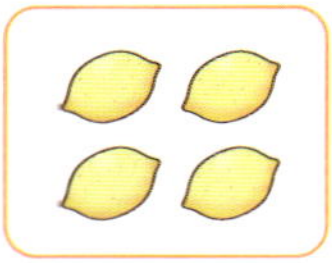

6

Learn to Write Numbers

Roll a hoop
and make a loop.
Just that quick
you've made a six.

Straight across and
down from heaven.
that's the way you
make a seven.

Application

Count the animals and write their numbers in the given space.

Learn to Write Numbers

Make an "S"
but don't you wait.
Go right back up
to make an eight.

Make a loop
And then a line.
That's a way to
make a nine.

Application

Find the missing number.

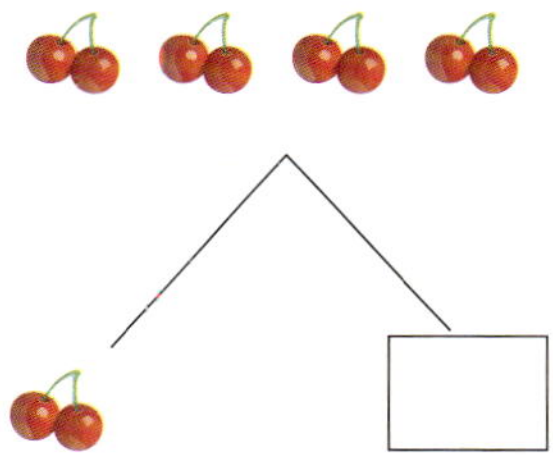

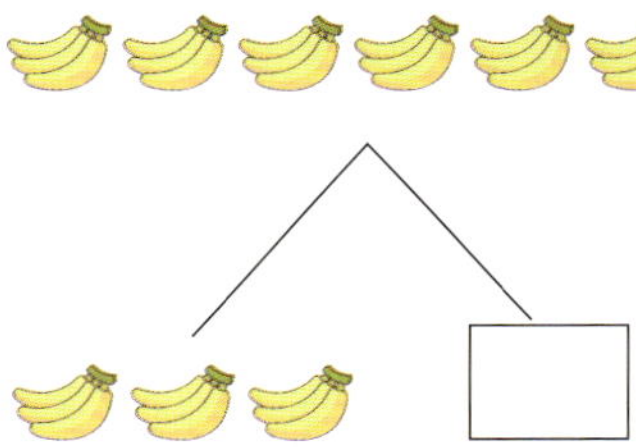

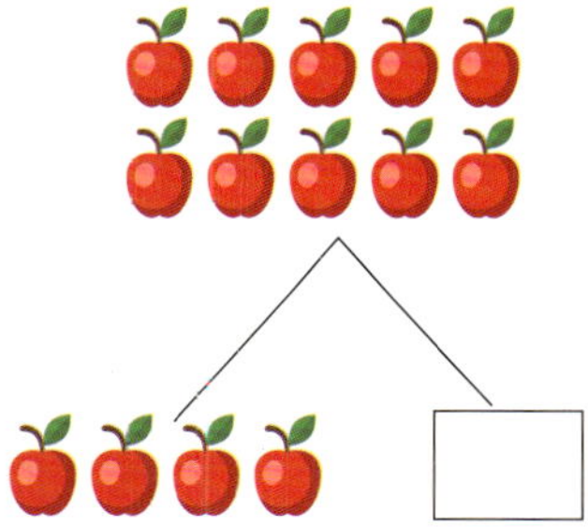

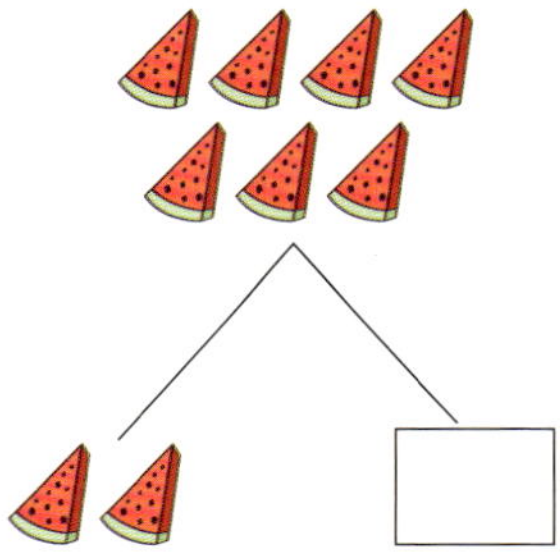

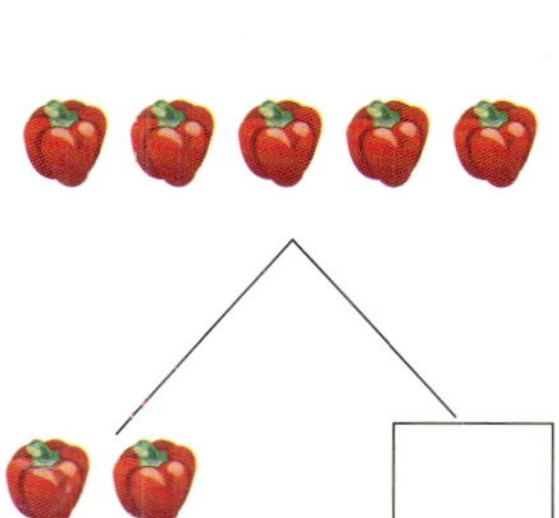

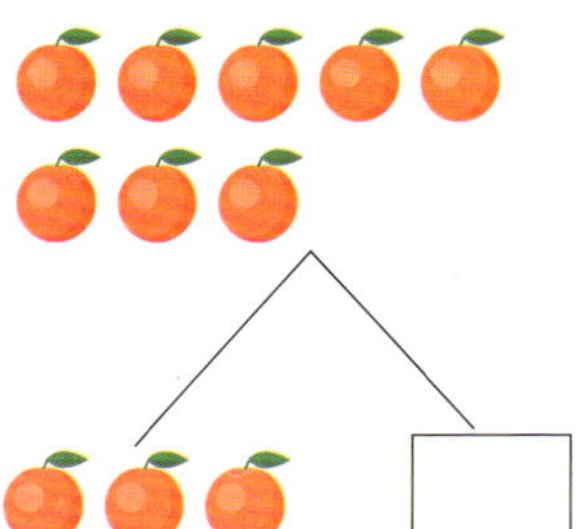

Learn to Write Numbers

one	one	one	one	one	one	one
two	two	two	two	two	two	two
three	three	three	three	three	three	three
four	four	four	four	four	four	four
five	five	five	five	five	five	five
six	six	six	six	six	six	six
seven	seven	seven	seven	seven	seven	seven
eight	eight	eight	eight	eight	eight	eight
nine	nine	nine	nine	nine	nine	nine
ten	ten	ten	ten	ten	ten	ten

Application

Count the fruits and write their total.

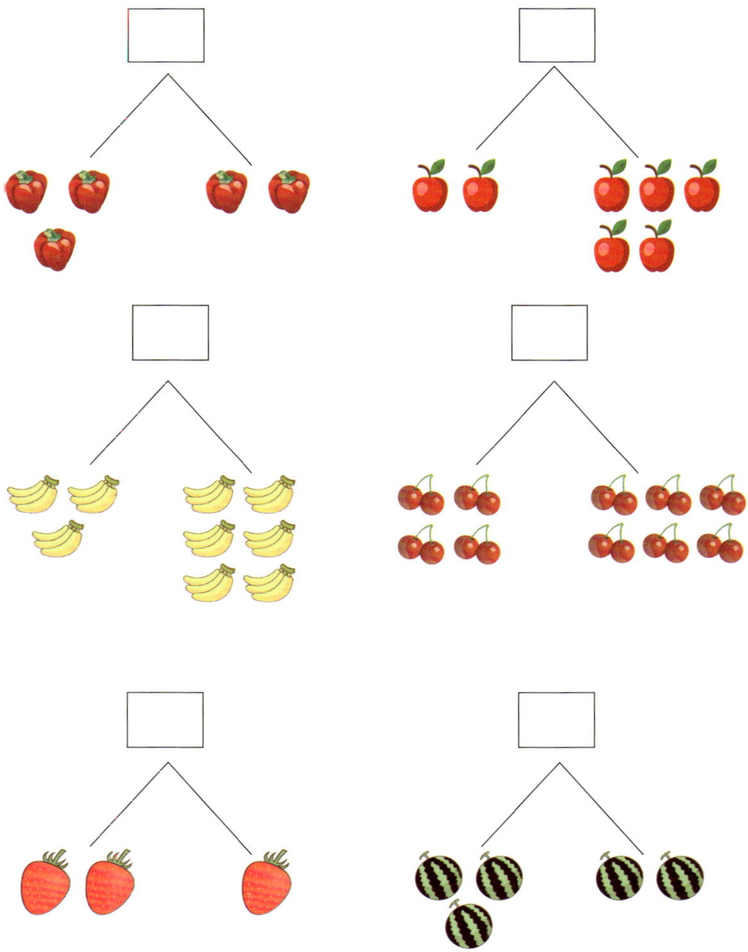

Learn to Write Numbers

0	0	0	0	0	0	0	0
1	1	1	1	1	1	1	1
2	2	2	2	2	2	2	2
3	3	3	3	3	3	3	3
4	4	4	4	4	4	4	4
5	5	5	5	5	5	5	5
6	6	6	6	6	6	6	6
7	7	7	7	7	7	7	7
8	8	8	8	8	8	8	8
9	9	9	9	9	9	9	9
10	11	12	13	14	15	16	17

Application

Count and Write.

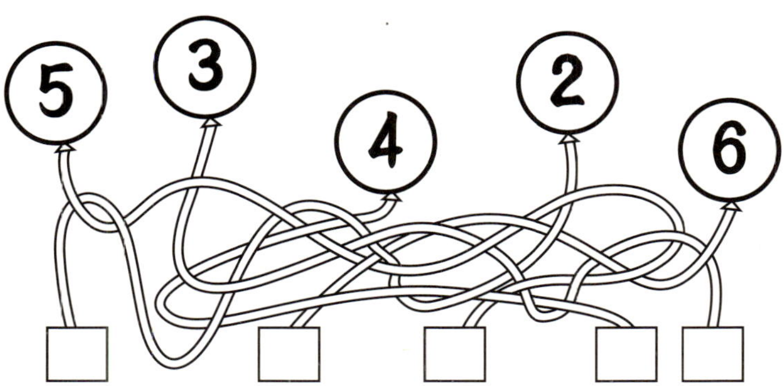

Learn to Write Numbers

18	19	20	21	22	23	24	25
26	27	28	29	30	31	32	33
34	35	36	37	38	39	40	41
42	43	44	45	46	47	48	49
50	51	52	53	54	55	56	57
58	59	60	61	62	63	64	65
66	67	68	69	70	71	72	73
74	75	76	77	78	79	80	81
82	83	84	85	86	87	88	89
90	91	92	93	94	95	96	97
98	99	10	01	00	10	01	00

Application

Count and write correct number of the fruits.

(Apple)

(Pear)

(Tangerine)

(Peach)

(   )Apple

(   )Pear

(   )Tangerine

(   )Peach

GOOD POSTURE

1. Both feet on the floor
2. Elbows off edge of desk
3. Sit back in the chair
4. Shoulders slightly forward
5. Proper desk height

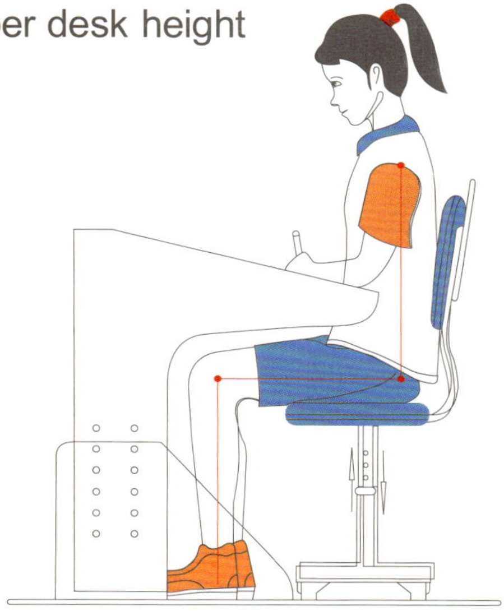

GOOD HANDWRITING

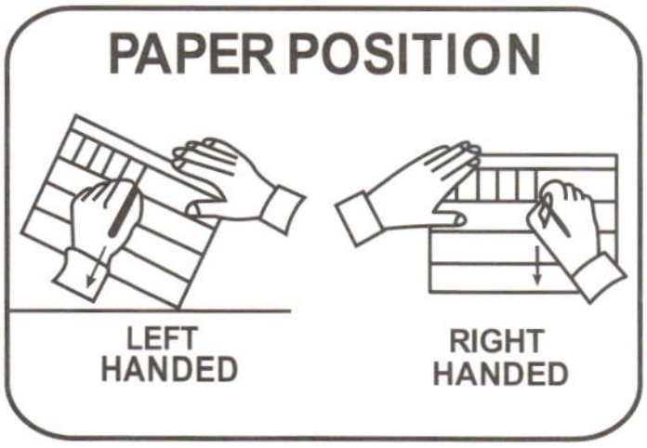

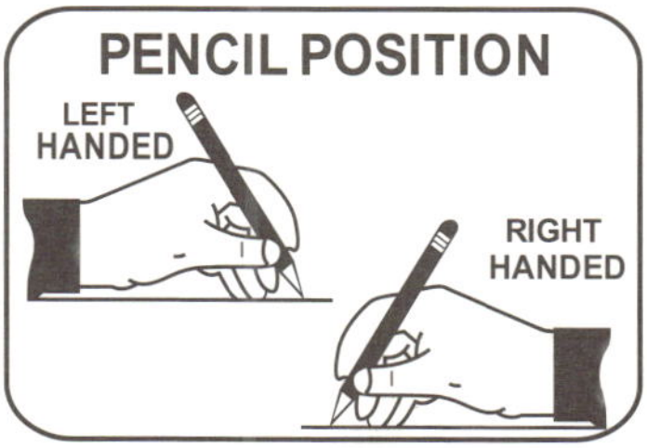

WONDER MAGIC NUMBERS

Practice Workbook For Preschoolers

Get ready to embark on a writing journey like no other! This interactive book for beginners with vanishing ink will inspire children to practice writing numbers repeatedly. The book allows beginners to enhance their handwriting skills by following the grooves to form perfect numbers.

Let the interactive book guide you to write confidently and have fun!

Titles in the series

Wonder House

Wonder House Books is an imprint of Prakash Books

UK £ 1.99 CAN $ 4.99 US $ 2.99

ISBN: 978-93-6214-989-3

9 789362 149893

Wonder House

MRP 00005900

www.wonderhousebooks.com